THE ARCHANGEL METHOD

Copyright © E the Medium

ISBN: 978-1-950080-18-2

All rights reserved. No part of this publication may be reproduced, distributed, or transmitted in any form or by any means, electronic or mechanical, including photocopying, recording, or by any information storage and retrieval system, without prior written permission from the copyright holder, except as permitted by law.

THE ARCHANGEL METHOD

E THE MEDIUM

CONTENTS

Chapter 1
THE POWER OF ANGELIC RITUAL
1

Chapter 2
MEET THE ARCHANGELS
5

Chapter 3
HOW TO USE THIS BOOK
13

Chapter 4
MAKE IT YOUR OWN
15

Chapter 5
THE RITUALS (1–78)
21

Chapter 6
CLOSING WORDS & YOUR NEXT STEP
43

Want More Support? Let's Connect
45

About Me
47

CHAPTER 1
THE POWER OF ANGELIC RITUAL

Have you ever felt like your desires are always just out of reach? As if there is something invisible standing between you and the life you're supposed to live?

You're not alone. As a Psychic Medium, I've done thousands of readings, and no matter who I'm reading, the patterns are always the same.

People feel stuck. They may be trapped in a financial situation, stuck in a loveless relationship, or stagnant in their career. Either way, happiness seems just out of reach. They become immobilized in fear and uncertainty.

They know what they want, but they don't know how to actually get there.

The same types of questions come up over and over again:

- "How do I find love that actually lasts?"
- "How do I stop sabotaging myself?"
- "How do I change my life when nothing ever seems to work?"

Sometimes, they just want to hear what they want, and the solution is right around the corner. They don't understand that the power for change is in their hands.

They don't want to look for themselves. I decided to teach people a clear way forward—a method they could use repeatedly to shift their energy and receive divine support for the things that matter most.

How do I know about it?

I was in the same boat, searching for an easy way out of my problems. Whether it was a personal issue, financial, or work-related, I learned that there are systems out there to help us regain control and achieve the peace and success we desire most.

This system has been thoroughly tested, proven, and has worked for my family, friends, and me.

That's why I created **The Archangel Method**: a system of 78 spiritual rituals designed to help you get unstuck and into alignment with what you truly want.

Each ritual is short, powerful, and easy to use.

Every single one is paired with an Archangel who specializes in the exact area needed for subjects on: love, healing, clarity, money, protection, purpose, peace, and more.

And yes, there are 78 rituals for a purpose.

Tarot became my link to the universe.

The number 78 mirrors the number of cards in a traditional Tarot deck. Tarot offers both grounded guidance and spiritual transformation.

Each ritual acts like a spiritual key that unlocks a new energy, helping you shift your mindset, clear emotional blocks, and call in what's been missing.

But here's the part that changes everything:

This method doesn't ask you to beg, wish, or hope.

Instead of saying "I want," or "Please bring this to me," every ritual begins with two powerful words:

"I Have."

That's the energetic difference between lack and alignment. When you say "I Have," you're stepping into the version of yourself that already lives with the outcome.

You're syncing up with the vibration of your desire and inviting the universe to meet you there.

So if you've ever wanted to:

- Cut ties with what's draining you.
- Open your heart to new love.
- Call in more money.
- Heal what's been holding you back.
- Or finally trust your own inner voice.

...you're in the right place.

So, join me on your journey to self-awareness and self-discovery.

CHAPTER 2
MEET THE ARCHANGELS

To work with angels, you don't need a title, a certification, or a long list of spiritual credentials. All you need is a willingness to connect and a belief that you're worthy of divine support. If you're reading this, you already have both.

In The Archangel Method, we work with 10 core Archangels. These are the spiritual heavy-hitters, each one holding a specific energetic key that aligns with the most common desires we experience in life.

You don't need to memorize a hundred names.

Just knowing these 10 and what they stand for is more than enough to shift your life.

Each ritual in this book has been matched to one of these Archangels. This was not a random matching.

It developed through repetition and channeling gained from thousands of readings.

These beings appear repeatedly in my readings, especially when specific themes emerge: healing, love, boundaries, clarity, abundance, and so on.

Here are the Archangels you'll be working with:

Archangel Michael

Keywords: Protection, confidence, courage, energetic boundaries, clearing fear.

When to Call on Michael: When you feel unsafe, overwhelmed, anxious, or drained by others. Michael helps you cut cords, reclaim your energy, and stand in your truth without worry.

How Michael Shows Up: A sudden feeling of strength. Seeing swords, shields, or the color blue. An urge to speak your truth without fear.

Archangel Raphael

Keywords: Healing, emotional release, grief, physical wellness, spiritual restoration.

When to Call on Raphael: When you're physically ill, emotionally weighed down, grieving, or seeking peace in your body and heart.

How Raphael Shows Up: Warmth in your chest, green light or imagery, synchronicities around health, or deep emotional release.

Archangel Gabriel

Keywords: Communication, creativity, parenting, inner truth, divine messages.

When to Call on Gabriel: When you're stuck expressing yourself, writing, speaking, or communicating in relationships. Also powerful for fertility and parenting.

How Gabriel Shows Up: Sudden clarity, strong urges to create or speak, dreams with written or spoken words, or angelic messages that repeat.

Archangel Uriel

Keywords: Wisdom, clarity, mindset, integration, daily life alignment.

When to Call on Uriel: When you're overthinking, doubting your direction, or needing grounded insight. Uriel turns divine messages into daily action.

How Uriel Shows Up: Mental breakthroughs, sudden insight, lightbulb moments, or recurring numbers and signs that guide your choices.

Archangel Chamuel

Keywords: Love, relationships, peace, emotional safety, connection.

When to Call on Chamuel: When you're seeking soulmate love, healing a relationship, or reconnecting with your inner self. Chamuel restores peace to the heart.

How Chamuel Shows Up: Soft pink energy, unexpected moments of calm, lightness, or intuition in the stomach area, bumping into someone "by chance."

Archangel Jophiel

Keywords: Joy, beauty, self-worth, perspective, mood shifts.

When to Call on Jophiel: When life feels heavy or dull, or when you need to see yourself or your situation through a lens of love and hope.

How Jophiel Shows Up: An uplift in mood, beauty in unexpected places, laughter, or yellow/golden hues.

Archangel Ariel

Keywords: Abundance, money, career, nature, manifestation.

When to Call on Ariel: When you're working on financial goals, manifesting material things, or need help with confidence in your career.

How Ariel Shows Up: Opportunities appearing, animals crossing your path, unexpected financial support, or feelings of grounded strength.

Archangel Haniel

Keywords: Intuition, emotional sensitivity, dreams, divine feminine flow.

When to Call on Haniel: When you want to enhance your intuition, honor your emotions, or reconnect with your inner knowing.

How Haniel Shows Up: Lunar energy, nighttime guidance, goosebumps, or deeply emotional dreams and synchronicities.

Archangel Zadkiel

Keywords: Forgiveness, compassion, past-life energy, emotional alchemy.

When to Call on Zadkiel: When you're holding resentment, guilt, or emotional pain from this or another lifetime. Zadkiel helps you alter the weight.

How Zadkiel Shows Up: Violet light, emotional clearing, recurring themes from the past, or old memories resurfacing for healing.

Archangel Metatron

Keywords: Life purpose, divine timing, spiritual development, higher self activation.

When to Call on Metatron: When you're going through a big life shift, feeling called to something greater, or stepping into your next level.

How Metatron Shows Up: Sacred geometry, time speeding up or slowing down, strong intuitive nudges, or pressure between the eyebrows.

These aren't just lofty ideas; these Archangels are deeply present and available. You don't have to "summon" them. It's much easier than that!

You just have to invite them in.

Say their name.

Speak your intention. Trust that they're already with you.

Throughout this book, each ritual will invoke one Archangel who governs that particular area. You'll speak in the present tense, using the phrase "I Have" to claim your desire as already real.

And when you do, something powerful happens: your energy rises, your nervous system softens, and your path begins to clear.

CHAPTER 3
HOW TO USE THIS BOOK

This isn't a book you read once and put on a shelf.

This is a book that will become part of your life.

Use it when you feel stuck, or when you're ready to shift something deep within you.

You don't need to follow it in order; you just need to follow your energy.

Each of the 78 rituals in this book is designed to meet you in a specific need, desire, or challenge. Flip through them and find the one that matches where you are or what you want to call in.

This is not about perfection. It's about connection.

You are not doing this alone. Every time you speak an "I Have" declaration, you are signaling to your angels that you are ready to receive. These are ancient rituals that have been used throughout the ages to aid humanity when it was needed. It's our way to reconnect with the Divine.

You're not begging. You're not chasing. You are choosing alignment, and they will respond to that.

You can work with one ritual at a time or create a small stack that addresses different areas of your life. For example:

- "I have soul-aligned love" (Chamuel)
- "I have clarity in my next steps" (Uriel)
- "I have money flowing to me with ease" (Ariel)

Repeat them together as a daily mantra or meditation. Let them reshape your energy and intention.

And remember: this method is powerful because it's simple.

You don't need to know everything about angels, tarot, or manifestation to get results here. All you need is willingness, openness, and a few minutes of presence.

The energy will shift when you do.

CHAPTER 4
MAKE IT YOUR OWN

This book includes 78 of the most common spiritual needs and desires.

The truth is: your life is one-of-a-kind. Sometimes, what you need won't be found in a list. That doesn't mean it's out of reach. It means it's time to co-create.

The Archangel Method isn't about following strict rules or memorizing prayers. It's about activating your connection with divine guidance. If you have a desire in your heart, you can turn it into a powerful ritual of your own.

This chapter shows you how.

This is where the real work begins, and it's also where things start to get beautifully simple. You've learned how the method works, who the Archangels are, and how to use the rituals. Now it's time to put it into action.

Inside this chapter, you'll find 78 "I Have" rituals, each one crafted to help you shift a specific desire or challenge into divine alignment.

You don't have to do them all at once. In fact, the power of this practice lies in tuning in to what you need right now.

Some people use these rituals as spiritual medicine, practicing them once a day, in the morning, to set the tone for their energy. Others return to the same few, again and again, as anchors. However you use them, just trust that your inner guidance and your angels will show you the way.

Each ritual includes:

- A specific desire or intention, written as an "I Have" declaration

- The Archangel best suited to help support that shift

- A short spoken ritual you can say aloud, write down, or meditate on

You can start anywhere in the list. Follow your intuition. Flip through until a title catches your attention. Or scan the table of contents when you're looking for help with something specific, like love, money, healing, clarity, protection, or emotional release.

Let these words be more than words. *Let them be activations.* You're not just reciting ideas. You're speaking yourself into alignment with what already exists for you in the spiritual realm and inviting it into form.

You're ready. Your angels are listening. Let's begin the rituals.

Your Personalized "I Have" Ritual

Here is a simple, repeatable process to create your own ritual for *any* desire, goal, or emotional shift you want to call in.

Step 1: Name Your Desire

Get clear about what you want. Use your own words. Write it down or say it out loud. It could be tangible ("I want to move to a new city") or emotional ("I want to feel confident and calm again").

Step 2: Choose an Archangel

Select the Archangel that best aligns with your intention. For a full description, refer to Chapter 2. Here are a few examples:

- **Michael**: for protection, courage, and cutting cords.
- **Raphael**: for healing and recovery.
- **Gabriel**: for communication, creativity, and being heard.
- **Ariel**: for abundance, money, and practical support.
- **Chamuel**: for love, relationships, and peace.
- **Haniel**: for intuition and emotional balance.
- **Jophiel**: for joy and self-worth.
- **Uriel**: for clarity, wisdom, and guidance.
- **Zadkiel**: for forgiveness and release.
- **Metatron**: for spiritual insight and big transitions.

If you don't know who to choose, trust your intuition. There's no wrong answer.

Step 3: Write Your "I Have" Declaration

Say it as if it's already real. Use simple, present-tense language.

Example:

"I have a peaceful, joyful home filled with love and light. Archangel Chamuel walks beside me as this becomes my reality. I am aligned, I am supported, and it is already done. Thank you, thank you, thank you."

Step 4: Feel It

Before or after you say your ritual, pause. Place your hand over your heart. Breathe. Imagine what it feels like to already have what you desire. Let the emotion rise within you.

This is the most important step. When you feel it, you signal to the Universe that you're already in alignment with the outcome.

Step 5: Repeat As Needed

You can say your ritual once or every day. You can whisper it before sleep or shout it in your car. Journal it. Meditate with it. There are no rules.

There are infinite things you can call in with this method:

- A raise at work.
- A better relationship with your body.
- Forgiveness for a past mistake.
- Trust in the unknown.
- Protection while you sleep.

This book does not limit you.

Your life is spread out before you and filled with limitless potential.

Let these 78 rituals guide you. Trust they will be there for you. Then, let your intuition take over.

You are not alone. Your angels are always listening.

CHAPTER 5
THE RITUALS (1–78)

Each of the following rituals is designed to bring your intention into alignment with the divine support of an Archangel. Use them as written or adapt them to your own voice.

The most important part is this: I implore to really feel as you are speaking your ritual. Feel the words, feel the emotions, feel that you have what you need. Feel it in your heart and mind as you speak it.

1. I Have Inner Peace — Archangel Chamuel

I have a calm, grounded peace within me. Archangel Chamuel surrounds me with soothing energy, and I feel safe in my body, heart, and mind. I am aligned, I am supported, and it is already done. Thank you, thank you, thank you.

2. I Have Financial Stability — Archangel Ariel

I have the money I need and more. Archangel Ariel opens the path to prosperity, guiding opportunities, ideas, and aligned action into my life. I am aligned, I am supported, and it is already done. Thank you, thank you, thank you.

3. I Have a Loving Relationship — Archangel Chamuel

I have a relationship that honors my soul and brings joy to my life. Archangel Chamuel gently leads me into divine partnership and deeper love. I am aligned, I am supported, and it is already done. Thank you, thank you, thank you.

4. I Have Clarity in My Purpose — Archangel Uriel

I have a clear sense of who I am and what I'm here to do. Archangel Uriel lights my path and helps me take action with confidence and insight. I am aligned, I am supported, and it is already done. Thank you, thank you, thank you.

5. I Have Vibrant Health — Archangel Raphael

I have energy, vitality, and wellness flowing through me. Archangel Raphael restores balance and healing in every part of my being. I am aligned, I am supported, and it is already done. Thank you, thank you, thank you.

6. I Have Creative Confidence — Archangel Gabriel

I have bold, beautiful creative energy flowing freely through me. Archangel Gabriel clears my blocks and inspires divine expression. I am aligned, I am supported, and it is already done. Thank you, thank you, thank you.

7. I Have Protection From Negative Energy — Archangel Michael

I have strong, divine protection surrounding me at all times. Archangel Michael shields my energy and helps me release fear and interference. I am aligned, I am supported, and it is already done. Thank you, thank you, thank you.

8. I Have Forgiveness in My Heart — Archangel Zadkiel

I have released old pain and made peace with the past. Archangel Zadkiel helps me let go with compassion so I can move forward freely. I am aligned, I am supported, and it is already done. Thank you, thank you, thank you.

9. I Have Strong Intuition — Archangel Haniel

I have access to my inner knowing and divine guidance. Archangel Haniel deepens my intuition and helps me trust my path. I am aligned, I am supported, and it is already done. Thank you, thank you, thank you.

10. I Have Joy in My Life — Archangel Jophiel

I have joy, laughter, and light all around me. Archangel Jophiel lifts my spirit and opens my eyes to beauty and blessings. I am aligned, I am supported, and it is already done. Thank you, thank you, thank you.

11. I Have Patience and Trust — Archangel Uriel

I have faith in divine timing and the process of life. Archangel Uriel keeps me grounded and wise as I wait with grace. I am aligned, I am supported, and it is already done. Thank you, thank you, thank you.

12. I Have Confidence in Myself
— Archangel Michael

I have unwavering confidence in who I am and what I offer. Archangel Michael fills me with strength and clarity. I am aligned, I am supported, and it is already done. Thank you, thank you, thank you.

13. I Have Healthy Boundaries
— Archangel Michael

I have clear, kind, and powerful boundaries that protect my energy. Archangel Michael helps me hold them with love. I am aligned, I am supported, and it is already done. Thank you, thank you, thank you.

14. I Have Courage to Begin Again
— Archangel Metatron

I have the bravery to start fresh and move forward. Archangel Metatron aligns my steps with divine timing. I am aligned, I am supported, and it is already done. Thank you, thank you, thank you.

15. I Have Divine Ideas Flowing Through Me — Archangel Gabriel

I have access to inspired ideas and creative downloads. Archangel Gabriel keeps my channels clear. I am aligned, I am supported, and it is already done. Thank you, thank you, thank you.

16. I Have Peace With My Body — Archangel Raphael

I have deep peace and gratitude for my body. Archangel Raphael nurtures my healing and self-love. I am aligned, I am supported, and it is already done. Thank you, thank you, thank you.

17. I Have Reconnection With My Loved One — Archangel Chamuel

I have meaningful reconnection and mutual understanding. Archangel Chamuel opens hearts and restores love. I am aligned, I am supported, and it is already done. Thank you, thank you, thank you.

18. I Have a Soul-Led Career — Archangel Ariel

I have a career that matches my soul's calling. Archangel Ariel guides me to abundance with meaning. I am aligned, I am supported, and it is already done. Thank you, thank you, thank you.

19. I Have Balance Between Work and Rest — Archangel Uriel

I have a life that honors both effort and ease. Archangel Uriel helps me stay in rhythm and alignment. I am aligned, I am supported, and it is already done. Thank you, thank you, thank you.

20. I Have Peace With What I Can't Control — Archangel Haniel

I have serenity even in the unknown. Archangel Haniel reminds me to surrender and trust the flow. I am aligned, I am supported, and it is already done. Thank you, thank you, thank you.

21. I Have Aligned Friendships — Archangel Chamuel

I have friendships that are uplifting, authentic, and aligned. Archangel Chamuel guides me toward loving connections. I am aligned, I am supported, and it is already done. Thank you, thank you, thank you.

22. I Have My Dream Home — Archangel Ariel

I have the perfect living space that supports and inspires me. Archangel Ariel aligns me with comfort, safety, and joy. I am aligned, I am supported, and it is already done. Thank you, thank you, thank you.

23. I Have Supportive Family Relationships — Archangel Raphael

I have peace and mutual respect in my family dynamics. Archangel Raphael heals old wounds and restores connection. I am aligned, I am supported, and it is already done. Thank you, thank you, thank you.

24. I Have Clarity in My Decisions — Archangel Uriel

I have the wisdom to make decisions with ease and alignment. Archangel Uriel lights my path with discernment and trust. I am aligned, I am supported, and it is already done. Thank you, thank you, thank you.

25. I Have Clear Communication — Archangel Gabriel

I have honest, loving communication that creates connection. Archangel Gabriel helps me speak from truth and love. I am aligned, I am supported, and it is already done. Thank you, thank you, thank you.

26. I Have Closure From My Past — Archangel Zadkiel

I have peace and understanding about what has been. Archangel Zadkiel helps me release old pain and make space for new joy. I am aligned, I am supported, and it is already done. Thank you, thank you, thank you.

27. I Have Freedom From Fear — Archangel Michael

I have freedom from the fears that once held me back. Archangel Michael cuts through illusions and restores my power. I am aligned, I am supported, and it is already done. Thank you, thank you, thank you.

28. I Have a Fresh Start — Archangel Metatron

I have a clean slate and a renewed spirit. Archangel Metatron helps me reset and realign with my purpose. I am aligned, I am supported, and it is already done. Thank you, thank you, thank you.

29. I Have Healing From Grief — Archangel Raphael

I have the space to grieve and the strength to heal. Archangel Raphael gently comforts and mends my heart. I am aligned, I am supported, and it is already done. Thank you, thank you, thank you.

30. I Have Motivation and Drive — Archangel Uriel

I have the energy and clarity to take action toward my goals. Archangel Uriel helps me stay focused and inspired. I am aligned, I am supported, and it is already done. Thank you, thank you, thank you.

31. I Have a Healthy Relationship With Food — Archangel Raphael

I have a nourishing and peaceful relationship with food. Archangel Raphael supports my body's wisdom and well-being. I am aligned, I am supported, and it is already done. Thank you, thank you, thank you.

32. I Have Support in My Parenting Journey — Archangel Gabriel

I have guidance, strength, and love as I parent. Archangel Gabriel helps me communicate with clarity and compassion. I am aligned, I am supported, and it is already done. Thank you, thank you, thank you.

33. I Have Divine Timing on My Side — Archangel Metatron

I have perfect timing in all that matters. Archangel Metatron aligns my path with what's right, when it's right. I am aligned, I am supported, and it is already done. Thank you, thank you, thank you.

34. I Have Room to Grieve and Grow — Archangel Zadkiel

I have space to feel and evolve through loss. Archangel Zadkiel helps me turn pain into deeper wisdom and love. I am aligned, I am supported, and it is already done. Thank you, thank you, thank you.

35. I Have Energy to Follow Through — Archangel Uriel

I have the energy and discipline to finish what I start. Archangel Uriel keeps me steady and focused. I am aligned, I am supported, and it is already done. Thank you, thank you, thank you.

36. I Have Release From Toxic Attachments — Archangel Michael

I have freedom from the people and patterns that drain me. Archangel Michael severs cords and strengthens my boundaries. I am aligned, I am supported, and it is already done. Thank you, thank you, thank you.

37. I Have Healing in My Marriage or Partnership — Archangel Chamuel

I have harmony, trust, and connection in my relationship. Archangel Chamuel restores love where it's been strained. I am aligned, I am supported, and it is already done. Thank you, thank you, thank you.

38. I Have a Peaceful Mind — Archangel Haniel

I have stillness and clarity within my thoughts. Archangel Haniel helps quiet the noise so I can hear divine guidance. I am aligned, I am supported, and it is already done. Thank you, thank you, thank you.

39. I Have Forgiven Myself — Archangel Zadkiel

I have compassion and grace for my past. Archangel Zadkiel helps me release shame and embrace who I am becoming. I am aligned, I am supported, and it is already done. Thank you, thank you, thank you.

40. I Have a Clear Vision for My Future — Archangel Uriel

I have clarity and direction about what's next. Archangel Uriel helps me dream with confidence and move forward with purpose. I am aligned, I am supported, and it is already done. Thank you, thank you, thank you.

41. I Have Alignment in My Career — Archangel Ariel

I have a career that reflects my truth and purpose. Archangel Ariel aligns me with meaningful work and steady success. I am aligned, I am supported, and it is already done. Thank you, thank you, thank you.

42. I Have Support in Starting My Business — Archangel Metatron

I have the clarity and momentum to begin. Archangel Metatron activates my purpose and draws the right people and resources. I am aligned, I am supported, and it is already done. Thank you, thank you, thank you.

43. I Have the Right People Around Me — Archangel Michael

I have relationships that are safe, inspiring, and aligned. Archangel Michael helps me release those who no longer match my path. I am aligned, I am supported, and it is already done. Thank you, thank you, thank you.

44. I Have Deep Self-Worth
— Archangel Jophiel

I have unshakable self-worth rooted in divine truth. Archangel Jophiel helps me see myself through the eyes of love. I am aligned, I am supported, and it is already done. Thank you, thank you, thank you.

45. I Have Trust in My Intuition
— Archangel Haniel

I have trust in the nudges, signs, and knowing within. Archangel Haniel helps me listen and act with faith. I am aligned, I am supported, and it is already done. Thank you, thank you, thank you.

46. I Have a Calm Nervous System
— Archangel Raphael

I have a body and mind that feel safe, centered, and at ease. Archangel Raphael soothes and regulates my energy. I am aligned, I am supported, and it is already done. Thank you, thank you, thank you.

47. I Have Peace in My Home — Archangel Chamuel

I have peace, love, and harmony within my home. Archangel Chamuel blesses my space with softness and connection. I am aligned, I am supported, and it is already done. Thank you, thank you, thank you.

48. I Have Clarity in My Messaging — Archangel Gabriel

I have a voice that is clear, true, and powerful. Archangel Gabriel guides my words and helps me express my mission. I am aligned, I am supported, and it is already done. Thank you, thank you, thank you.

49. I Have Freedom From Comparison — Archangel Jophiel

I have confidence in my unique journey. Archangel Jophiel helps me focus on my joy instead of others' paths. I am aligned, I am supported, and it is already done. Thank you, thank you, thank you.

50. I Have a Strong Connection With Spirit — Archangel Haniel

I have a vibrant and steady link to the divine. Archangel Haniel helps me stay attuned to spiritual insight and presence. I am aligned, I am supported, and it is already done. Thank you, thank you, thank you.

51. I Have Peace With My Past
— Archangel Zadkiel

I have acceptance and understanding of everything that came before. Archangel Zadkiel helps me soften the past and reclaim my power. I am aligned, I am supported, and it is already done. Thank you, thank you, thank you.

52. I Have a Successful Launch
— Archangel Ariel

I have a launch that flows with ease, visibility, and abundance. Archangel Ariel blesses my work with traction and trust. I am aligned, I am supported, and it is already done. Thank you, thank you, thank you.

53. I Have Flow and Ease in My Life — Archangel Haniel

I have a life that feels supported, spacious, and graceful. Archangel Haniel guides me to surrender and divine rhythm. I am aligned, I am supported, and it is already done. Thank you, thank you, thank you.

54. I Have Peace During Change
— Archangel Michael

I have strength and calm as things shift around me. Archangel Michael grounds me and clears fear from my path. I am aligned, I am supported, and it is already done. Thank you, thank you, thank you.

55. I Have Emotional Resilience — Archangel Raphael

I have the capacity to feel deeply and still rise. Archangel Raphael helps me move through emotions with healing and grace. I am aligned, I am supported, and it is already done. Thank you, thank you, thank you.

56. I Have a Deeper Connection to My Gifts — Archangel Metatron

I have full access to my spiritual gifts and soul wisdom. Archangel Metatron helps me integrate and trust what I carry. I am aligned, I am supported, and it is already done. Thank you, thank you, thank you.

57. I Have Harmony in My Community — Archangel Chamuel

I have a community built on respect, joy, and support. Archangel Chamuel brings people together in love and purpose. I am aligned, I am supported, and it is already done. Thank you, thank you, thank you.

58. I Have Breakthroughs in My Healing — Archangel Raphael

I have big, beautiful shifts in my healing journey. Archangel Raphael helps me release layers and find peace. I am aligned, I am supported, and it is already done. Thank you, thank you, thank you.

59. I Have Ease in My Manifestation — Archangel Ariel

I have the ability to manifest with clarity and flow. Archangel Ariel aligns me with tangible support for my desires. I am aligned, I am supported, and it is already done. Thank you, thank you, thank you.

60. I Have Divine Perspective on My Challenges — Archangel Uriel

I have wisdom beyond the moment. Archangel Uriel helps me see challenges as part of a larger purpose. I am aligned, I am supported, and it is already done. Thank you, thank you, thank you.

61. I Have Closure With Someone From My Past — Archangel Zadkiel

I have peace and release from past relationships. Archangel Zadkiel helps me lovingly close that chapter so I can move forward. I am aligned, I am supported, and it is already done. Thank you, thank you, thank you.

62. I Have a Deep Connection With My Children — Archangel Gabriel

I have open, loving, and respectful communication with my children. Archangel Gabriel helps me nurture their hearts and mine. I am aligned, I am supported, and it is already done. Thank you, thank you, thank you.

63. I Have Motivation to Take Action — Archangel Uriel

I have clear energy and divine fire that moves me forward. Archangel Uriel keeps me focused and energized for aligned action. I am aligned, I am supported, and it is already done. Thank you, thank you, thank you.

64. I Have a Soft Heart Without Losing My Power — Archangel Michael

I have both tenderness and strength. Archangel Michael helps me lead with love while honoring my boundaries. I am aligned, I am supported, and it is already done. Thank you, thank you, thank you.

65. I Have Peace With a Loss I Experienced — Archangel Raphael

I have healing around the grief I carry. Archangel Raphael gently supports my heart as I find meaning in the sorrow. I am aligned, I am supported, and it is already done. Thank you, thank you, thank you.

66. I Have Room for New Love — Archangel Chamuel

I have space in my heart for a new, aligned connection. Archangel Chamuel prepares the way with clarity and grace. I am aligned, I am supported, and it is already done. Thank you, thank you, thank you.

67. I Have the Right Clients and Audience — Archangel Ariel

I have people who are ready and eager to receive my work. Archangel Ariel magnetizes those who are aligned with my message. I am aligned, I am supported, and it is already done. Thank you, thank you, thank you.

68. I Have a Peaceful Morning Routine — Archangel Haniel

I have mornings filled with stillness, flow, and intuitive alignment. Archangel Haniel helps me begin each day connected to Spirit. I am aligned, I am supported, and it is already done. Thank you, thank you, thank you.

69. I Have the Courage to Be Seen — Archangel Gabriel

I have the confidence to share my truth and shine publicly. Archangel Gabriel helps me step forward with clarity and heart. I am aligned, I am supported, and it is already done. Thank you, thank you, thank you.

70. I Have Clarity Around a Big Decision — Archangel Uriel

I have inner certainty and divine insight. Archangel Uriel reveals what's true and lights my next step. I am aligned, I am supported, and it is already done. Thank you, thank you, thank you.

71. I Have a Strong Connection With My Angels — Archangel Haniel

I have an open, trusting relationship with my angelic guides. Archangel Haniel deepens my connection and keeps the channels clear. I am aligned, I am supported, and it is already done. Thank you, thank you, thank you.

72. I Have Momentum in My Business — Archangel Metatron

I have traction, clarity, and divine alignment in my business. Archangel Metatron moves energy and opens the doors. I am aligned, I am supported, and it is already done. Thank you, thank you, thank you.

73. I Have Divine Help in Letting Go — Archangel Michael

I have support in releasing what no longer serves me. Archangel Michael clears attachments and strengthens my will. I am aligned, I am supported, and it is already done. Thank you, thank you, thank you.

74. I Have Restful Sleep and Protection at Night — Archangel Raphael

I have peace and rejuvenation each night. Archangel Raphael watches over my body and dreams while I rest deeply. I am aligned, I am supported, and it is already done. Thank you, thank you, thank you.

75. I Have Protection Over My Children and Loved Ones — Archangel Michael

I have divine guardianship over the ones I love. Archangel Michael surrounds them with safety, strength, and peace. I am aligned, I am supported, and it is already done. Thank you, thank you, thank you.

76. I Have Support While Navigating Change — Archangel Uriel

I have steady guidance through transition. Archangel Uriel helps me stay rooted while life reshapes around me. I am aligned, I am supported, and it is already done. Thank you, thank you, thank you.

77. I Have Gratitude in My Heart — Archangel Jophiel

I have a deep appreciation for the blessings in my life. Archangel Jophiel helps me see beauty in the small and sacred. I am aligned, I am supported, and it is already done. Thank you, thank you, thank you.

78. I Have Everything I Need — Archangel Ariel

I have enough, I am enough, and all is in divine order. Archangel Ariel grounds me in the abundance of now. I am aligned, I am supported, and it is already done. Thank you, thank you, thank you.

CHAPTER 6
CLOSING WORDS & YOUR NEXT STEP

You've made it.

You've met the Archangels.

You've learned how to work with them.

And you now have 78 powerful rituals to shift your energy and change your life.

But this isn't the end.

This is your invitation to *keep going*.

Because spiritual growth isn't a finish line. It's a relationship — with yourself, with the divine, and with the life you're here to live. The more you show up for this work, the more support, guidance, and miracles you'll feel unfolding around you.

The rituals you've read aren't just nice affirmations or comforting words. They're energetic declarations. You're not just asking. You're claiming. You're co-creating.

So now, it's your turn.

Use this book like a spiritual tool. Flip to a ritual every morning. Choose one when you're feeling stuck. Repeat the same one daily until you feel the shift.

Feel free to make it your own. Don't feel limited by what's here. These 78 "I Have" rituals are a starting point. The possibilities are endless. If there's something else you want to bring into your life, write your own declaration. Choose the Archangel who matches the energy. Trust what comes through.

Let this method become a way of life. You don't have to be a psychic or healer to work with angels. You just have to show up. Keep connecting. Keep declaring. Keep trusting.

WANT MORE SUPPORT? LET'S CONNECT

If this book spoke to you — if it helped you shift, open, or remember what's possible — I'd love to hear from you.

Whether you're looking for:

- A 1:1 private psychic or mediumship reading.
- Social Media Coaching.
- A custom ritual.
- Or to just say hello…

You can reach me directly at ethemedium@gmail.com

@ethemedium – www.ethemedium.com

Find me on TikTok where I go live almost daily and preform FREE readings.

ABOUT ME

Hi, I'm E — but on TikTok, other social platforms and in the spiritual world, people know me as **E The Medium**.

I've done thousands of readings for people around the world. I use a mix of tarot and my own intuition. I connect with angels. I hear from passed-on loved ones. And I help people find peace, clarity, and direction — especially when they feel stuck.

Over the years, I noticed a pattern:

No matter who I was reading, people were all asking the same kinds of questions…

"How do I bring this person back into my life?"

"How do I find love that doesn't hurt?"

"How do I make more money doing what I love?"

"How do I finally let go of what's weighing me down?"

This book is my answer to all of that.

The Archangel Method is a way for you to stop wondering and start doing. It gives you the tools to claim what you desire — and to get divine support while doing it.

You're not alone.

You never were.

And now, you have a method.